MW00720797

by Pauline Cartwright
illustrated by Kate Ashforth

Harcourt

SCHOOL PUBLISHERS

ISBN 10: 0-15-350397-1
ISBN 13: 978-0-15-350397-9

Ordering Options
ISBN 10: 0-15-350332-7 (Grade 2 Below-Level Collection)
ISBN 13: 978-0-15-350332-0 (Grade 2 Below-Level Collection)
ISBN 10: 0-15-357424-0 (package of 5)
ISBN 13: 978-0-15-357424-5 (package of 5)

1 2 3 4 5 6 7 8 9 10   179   15 14 13 12 11 10 09 08 07 06

Penny played with AJ every day.
AJ was nine, and Penny was only seven.

AJ was better at catching
than Penny.

AJ ran faster than Penny.

AJ danced better than
Penny.

AJ's dad decided to take the girls swimming.

"I can swim fast," said AJ, as they drove past the police station.

"Please stand by the sign
while I buy the tickets,"
said Dad.
"I can swim very fast,"
said AJ.

"Prove it!" said Penny.
AJ and Penny slid into the
water.

Penny went around eight times without stopping!

Penny could swim better
than AJ.
AJ climbed out.

"Did you already know
Penny was good?" AJ asked
Dad.
"Yes," he said with a smile.

"We are all good at
something," he added.
Penny got out of the water.
Dad and AJ clapped for
Penny.

Think Critically

1. How old were AJ and Penny?

2. What could AJ do better than Penny?

3. What words would you use to describe Dad? Why?

4. How did you feel when Penny swam much better than AJ?

5. What message do you think the author was trying to give readers?

⭐ Language Arts

Chart Write the names of three friends across the top of a sheet of paper. Underneath write what each friend is good at.

 School-Home Connection Tell someone at home about what Dad said to AJ. Discuss what each person in your family is good at.